THIRD GR...
MAIN IDEA AND DETAILS

A WORKBOOK TO
BUILD READING SKILLS

ISBN 9798873861248

First printing edition 2024.

10 9 8 7 6 5 4 3 2 1

Published in Ormond Beach, Florida.

Contact the author :
fishyrobb.com

Penguin Homes

Many people believe that all penguins live in the frigid climate of Antarctica but that's not true. Penguins live in many places all throughout the Southern Hemisphere. Some even live in warmer climates.

Only two species of penguin live in Antarctica. Those are the Emperor and the Adélie penguins. Other penguins live along the coasts of Australia and New Zealand. The warmest penguin home of all is the Galápagos Islands. These islands are located near the equator in the warmest part of the world. Penguins can survive there due to the cold ocean waters in that area.

Directions: Read the passage. Answer each question. Underline where you found the answers in the text.

1. All penguins live in cold areas.

    a) true   b) false

2. Name 3 specific locations where penguins live:

    _____

    _____

    _____

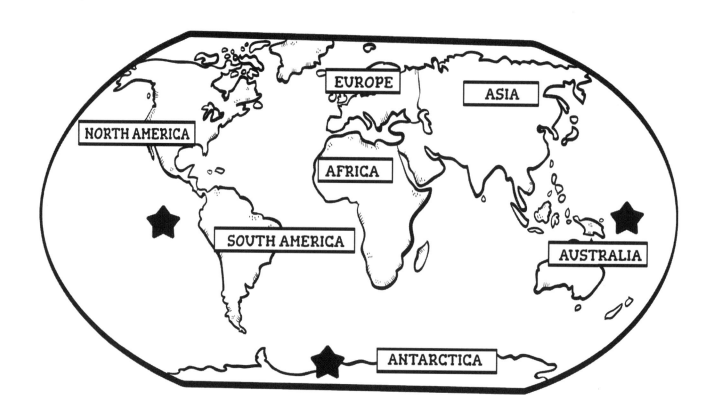

Research Challenge

What species of penguin live
in the Galapagos Islands?

Directions: Think about the passage you read. What was the most important idea? Complete the chart:

Supporting Details

Main Idea

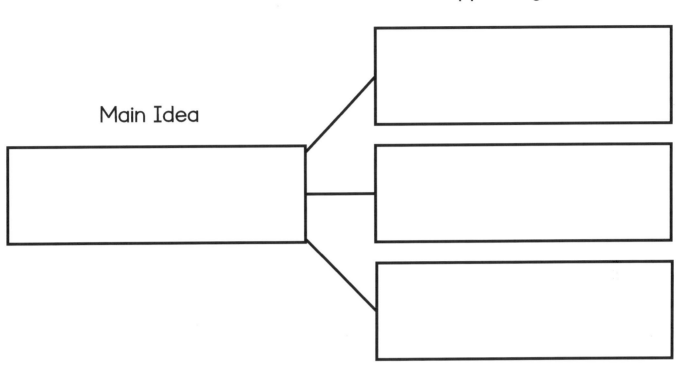

 Cut out the statements.

 Glue them on the chart above to show which is the main idea and which are details..

Other penguins live along the coasts of Australia and New Zealand.

Only two species of penguin live in Antarctica.

The warmest penguin home of all is the Galápagos Islands.

Penguins live in many places throughout the Southern Hemisphere.

Dental Health

How many teeth have you lost? Did you know that once your adult teeth grow in, they have to last the rest of your life? That's why it's so important to take good care of your teeth and gums!

Unlike other body parts, a tooth usually can't repair itself. If you get a cavity, a dentist must remove the decayed part and put a filling in its place. That is why it's so important to brush your teeth every day. You also need to take care of your gums. If they get infected, you can lose your teeth. Brushing and flossing daily will keep your gums healthy and prevent halitosis, or bad breath. No one wants dragon breath! These are some reasons you should care for your teeth.

Directions: Read the passage. Answer each question. Underline where you found the answers in the text.

1. A tooth doesn't usually repair itself.

   a) true   b) false

2. What can you do to prevent halitosis?

   _____

   _____

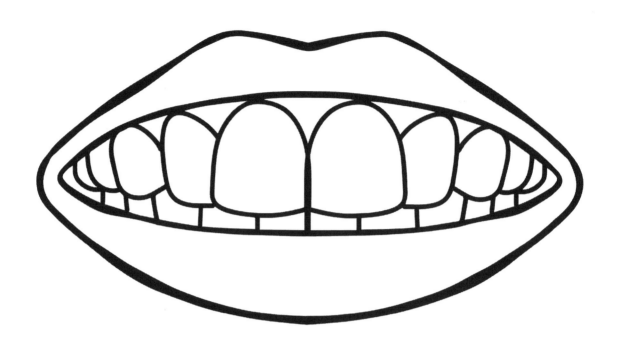

Research Challenge

How many teeth do children have?

What about adults?

Directions: Think about the passage you read. What was the most important idea? Complete the chart:

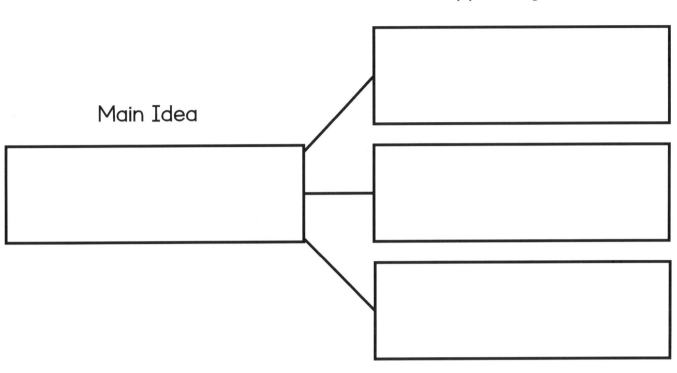

Supporting Details

Main Idea

 Cut out the statements.

 Glue them on the chart above to show which is the main idea and which are details..

It is important to take good care of your teeth and gums.

Brushing and flossing will keep your gums healthy and prevent halitosis.

If your gums get infected, you can lose your teeth.

Unlike other body parts, a tooth usually can't repair itself.

Our Sun

Everyone knows that the sun gives us light. But did you know that the sun makes life possible? Every living thing on Earth relies on the sun.

The sun produces heat that keeps the Earth at the correct temperature. Without the sun, all of the water on Earth would be frozen. Plants and animals must have water to survive. Plants also need sunlight to form glucose which they use for food. As a plant produces glucose, it gives off oxygen. This is released into the air for us to breathe. Finally, the sun creates gravity that keeps the Earth and all of the other planets in orbit. Without the sun, our solar system would not exist.

Directions: Read the passage. Answer each question. Underline where you found the answers in the text.

1. The sun gives off oxygen.

   a) true   b) false

2. Explain a way plants use sunlight that helps humans:

   _____

   _____

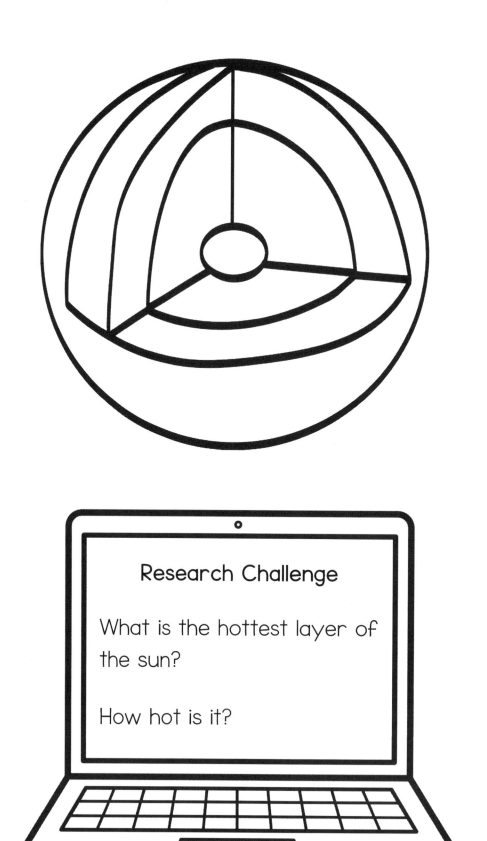

Research Challenge

What is the hottest layer of the sun?

How hot is it?

Directions: Think about the passage you read. What was the most important idea? Complete the chart:

Supporting Details

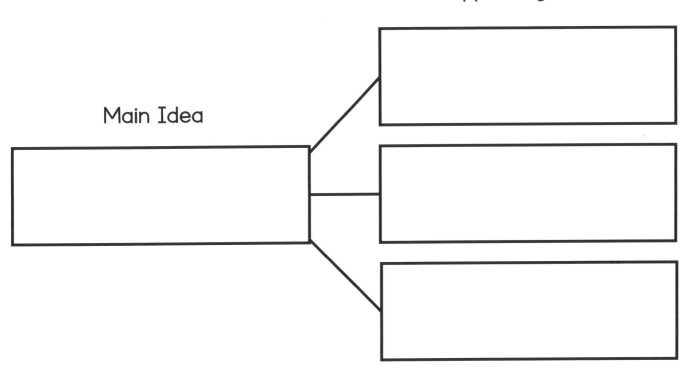

Main Idea

 Cut out the statements.

 Glue them on the chart above to show which is the main idea and which are details..

Without the sun, all the water on Earth would be frozen.

Life on Earth would not be possible without the sun.

The sun creates gravity that keeps the Earth and all of the other planets in orbit.

Plants need sunlight to produce glucose which they use for food.

Pioneer Life

Today, most children go to school during the day and play with their friends when they get home. On the weekend, they might participate in sports, go to the movies, or play video games. But life was not like that during pioneer times.

Many pioneer children learned at home instead of going to school. They woke up early and had to help with chores most of the day. Girls helped cook, clean, and sew, and took care of younger siblings. Boys helped their fathers chop wood, build, hunt, and farm. Unlike today, there was no television or video games. Pioneer children had to make their own fun – but only after their work was done.

Directions: Read the passage. Answer each question. Underline where you found the answers in the text.

1. Most pioneer children were schooled at home.

   a) true   b) false

2. What sentence shows that in pioneer times work came before play?

   _____

   _____

   _____

Research Challenge

What are some foods the pioneers ate on the Oregon Trail?

Directions: Think about the passage you read. What was the most important idea? Complete the chart:

Supporting Details

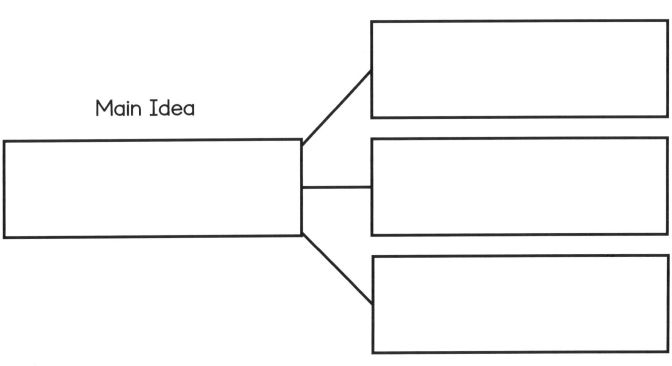

Main Idea

 Cut out the statements.

 Glue them on the chart above to show which is the main idea and which are details..

Many pioneer children learned at home instead of going to school.

They had to wake up early and help with chores most of the day.

Unlike today, there was no television or video games.

Childhood during pioneer times was very different than it is today.

Helen Keller

When Helen Keller was born, she was a strong and healthy baby. But as a young child, Helen fell ill. The sickness left her blind and deaf. Learning was difficult for Helen. She could not communicate at all.

A woman named Anne Sullivan became her teacher. With Anne's help, Helen learned to use a special kind of sign language. She also learned to read Braille. Helen was a fast learner. She eventually went to college and was the first deaf-blind person to earn a bachelor's degree. She also learned four languages. As an adult, Helen wrote many books and spoke out about the rights of disabled people. Helen became an inspiration for many.

Directions: Read the passage. Answer each question. Underline where you found the answers in the text.

1. Helen was born blind.

   a) true   b) false

2. What did Helen achieve that had never been done by a deaf and blind person?

   _____

   _____

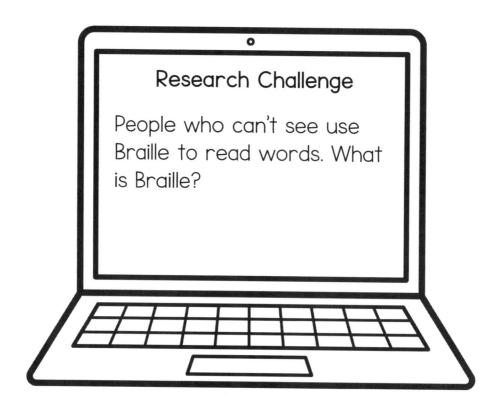

Research Challenge

People who can't see use Braille to read words. What is Braille?

Directions: Think about the passage you read. What was the most important idea? Complete the chart:

Supporting Details

Main Idea

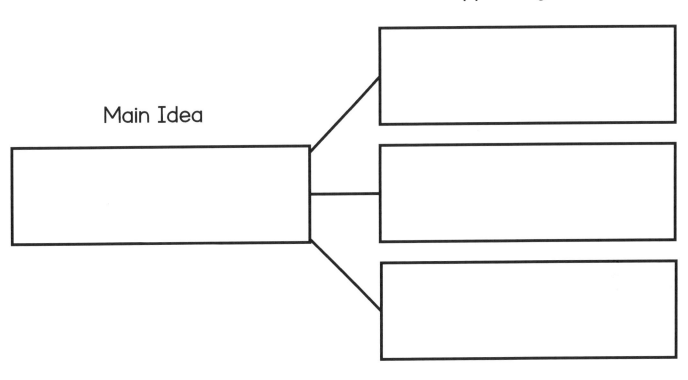

 Cut out the statements.

 Glue them on the chart above to show which is the main idea and which are details..

Helen learned a special kind of sign language and how to read Braille.

Helen Keller overcame her disability and became an inspiration to others.

Helen wrote many books and spoke out about the rights of the disabled.

She also learned four languages.

Directions: Read each passage. Underline or highlight the detail that does not support the main idea.

Main Idea: Dolphins are mammals.

You might think a dolphin is a kind of fish but it is actually a mammal. Dolphins have lungs just like you. They must come to the surface to breathe air. A baby dolphin, called a calf, drinks its mother's milk. Dolphins are warm-blooded animals, while fish are cold-blooded. Dolphins can also swim up to 20 miles per hour. Finally, dolphins have a small amount of hair on their bodies.

Main Idea: Many products can be made from corn.

Corn is one of the most popular vegetables to eat, but it can be used for more than just food. Corn is an ingredient in many everyday products like glue and lipstick. It is used to make ethanol which is added to gasoline. However, ethanol is not good for the environment. Hand soaps and toothpaste both have corn-based ingredients. Believe it or not, corn is even used in the production of baby diapers!

Directions: Read each passage. Underline or highlight the detail that does not support the main idea.

Main Idea: Spiders are not insects.

Many people are surprised to learn that spiders are arachnids, not insects. They are different in several ways. An insect has six legs while spiders have eight. Spiders live on every continent except Antarctica. Although most insects have wings and can fly, spiders do not. Another difference is the number of body parts. Insects have three while spiders only have two.

Main Idea: Sofia is a talented musician.

Some people know how to play an instrument but my friend, Sofia, can play four. She plays flute, cello, piano, and guitar. She also sings in the school chorus and writes her own music. Last year, Sofia won the school talent show when she sang one of the songs she wrote. Besides performing, Sofia also gives lessons to her friends. Even though she is busy, Sofia still makes time for her favorite sport, soccer.

Directions: Read each passage. Underline or highlight the detail that does not support the main idea.

Main Idea: Benjamin Franklin was a great inventor.

Benjamin Franklin, one of our founding fathers, was also an inventor. Franklin lived in Philadelphia, Pennsylvania. One of his inventions that is used by many people today is bifocal eye-glasses. He also invented a stove for cooking, and swimming paddles that are similar to swim fins. Have you ever noticed the odometer in your parent's car that tells how far you've driven? That's a Ben Franklin invention too!

Main Idea: Sacagawea helped Lewis and Clark on their journey.

When Lewis and Clark explored the west for President Jefferson, they took along a young Native American named Sacagawea. She helped translate for them when they met Indian tribes. She also helped guide the explorers through the mountains along paths she knew well. Sacagawea had a baby during the expedition. When the group needed more horses, Sacagawea arranged to buy them from her brother, the tribe's chief.

Directions: Read each passage. Underline or highlight the detail that does not support the main idea.

Main Idea: Logan is afraid of heights.

My brother, Logan, is afraid of heights. He starts to shake whenever we have to ride in an elevator. He avoids climbing on ladders, even to get on my bunk bed. Logan misses a lot of fun because of his fear. He refuses to ride the Ferris wheel or roller coaster at the fair. He will not climb trees with me and our friends. He has been afraid of heights since he was three years old. Logan is two years younger than me.

Main Idea: The hippopotamus is extremely dangerous.

Did you know that the hippopotamus is the most dangerous land animal in Africa? They are huge, aggressive, and territorial. A hippo can run up to 30 miles per hour and will charge anyone who threatens it. Their huge teeth, weighing six pounds each, can easily crush anything they bite. Hippos are herbivores and eat only plants. Almost 3,000 people are killed by wild hippos each year.

Directions: Read each passage. Underline or highlight the detail that does not support the main idea.

Main Idea: Car racing requires a lot of safety equipment.

Racecar drivers must protect themselves by using proper safety equipment. Otherwise, a high-speed accident can be deadly. Racing is an exciting sport! A helmet protects the driver's head and face. A special fireproof suit and gloves are worn in case the car catches fire. Today, race cars are equipped with HANS devices. This is a special harness that keeps the head and neck still during a wreck.

Main Idea: Video games have changed a lot over the years..

Kids in the early 1970s had to visit an arcade to play video games. Home video games didn't exist until a few years later. One of the first home games was called Pong. It was very simple compared to the games of today. Players had to hit a little ball with a paddle. Video games now are much more advanced. Many of them look like movies with lifelike characters and actions. Super Mario is a very popular game for kids.

Directions: Read each passage. Underline or highlight the detail that does not support the main idea.

Main Idea: The U.S. has three branches of government.

The United States government is divided into three main parts called branches. The legislative branch creates our laws. The judicial branch interprets our laws. The executive branch enforces them. A system of checks and balances makes sure these three branches have equal power and work together. In the United States, adults have the right to vote. All three parts of our government are based in Washington D.C.

Main Idea: Disney World is a popular vacation spot.

Every year more than 20 million people visit the Magic Kingdom at Disney World. Some of them travel thousands of miles to spend their vacation at "The Happiest Place on Earth." Disney World opened in Florida in 1971. It is the most visited amusement park in the world. People of all ages love the rides and shows which makes it the ideal spot for a family trip. Some people even go back more than once!

Camping

Main Idea	Main Idea	Main Idea
It's important to bring the right equipment when you go camping.	Camping is a perfect activity for people who like outdoor recreation.	Camping in a tent is better than using a camper.

Cut out the statements below. Glue them under the main idea that they support on the chart above.

Many campsites are near lakes or rivers where you can fish or swim.	It's more expensive to rent a site with camper hookups than it is a tent.	You can fit a tent right into your car trunk.
If you plan to cook over a fire, be sure to have matches or a lighter.	It can be very dark in the woods at night, so you will want a flashlight.	There are many kinds of birds at a campsite for bird watchers to enjoy.
Sleeping in a tent is almost like sleeping outside.	You can go hiking during the day to see nature and get some exercise.	There can be a lot of insects around, so don't forget bug repellant.

Bees

Main Idea	Main Idea	Main Idea
A hive has several types of bees that perform different jobs..	Bees can be a valuable part of a farm.	Not all bees are dangerous.

Cut out the statements below. Glue them under the main idea that they support on the chart above.

Carpenter bees are very large, but the males can't sting.	Most bees are not aggressive. They only sting if you disturb them.	For many crops to grow, the flowers must first be pollinated by bees.
Some worker bees are nurses who take care of newly hatched larvae.	Bees produce honey that can be sold at the market.	Some species of bees have a very small stinger that doesn't even work.
Drones are male bees that mate with the queen.	Bees pollinate clover and and other plants that are grown to feed livestock.	Collecting food and taking care of the hive is done by worker bees.

Pets

Main Idea	Main Idea	Main Idea
Some pets are easier to care for than others.	A pet can be more than just a friend.	Having a pet is good for your health.

Cut out the statements below. Glue them under the main idea that they support on the chart above.

Dogs need to be trained, walked, and groomed regularly.	Pets can help you relax and give you a feeling of well-being.	Cats are very easy to litter box train and don't mind being left alone.
Pets can be trained to help the disabled with everyday tasks.	Betta fish need just a small bowl and a sprinkle of food each day.	A pet can help protect your home from intruders.
Dogs are often used to guard livestock on farms and ranches.	Children with pets have a lower chance of having allergies.	Having a pet has been proven to lower your blood pressure.

Stars

Main Idea	Main Idea	Main Idea
The sun is the center of our solar system.	Scientists use special tools to study stars.	There are different types of stars.

Cut out the statements below. Glue them under the main idea that they support on the chart above.

Astronomers long ago and today use star charts to map star locations.	A reflector telescope bounces starlight through mirrors.	Our sun is not the largest or hottest star. It is a medium size yellow star.
The largest star, called a hypergiant, is 1,700 times bigger than our sun.	All the planets in our solar system revolve around one star – our sun.	The planets get heat and light from the sun. Its gravity holds them in place.
It takes Earth 365 days to orbit the sun. Jupiter takes 12 years!	Stars can be blue, white, yellow, or red. Blue stars are the hottest.	Radio telescopes use radio waves to show stars in great detail.

ANSWER KEYS

Penguin Homes

Many people believe that all penguins live in the frigid climate of Antarctica but that's not true. Penguins live in many places all throughout the Southern Hemisphere. <u>Some even live in warmer climates.</u>

Only two species of penguin live in Antarctica. Those are the Emperor and the Adélie penguins. <u>Other penguins live along the coasts of Australia and New Zealand. The warmest penguin home of all is the Galápagos Islands.</u> These islands are located near the equator in the warmest part of the world. Penguins can survive there due to the cold ocean waters in that area.

Directions: Read the passage. Answer each question. Underline where you found the answers in the text.

1. All penguins live in cold areas.

    a) true   (b) false)

2. Name 3 specific locations where penguins live:

    <u>coast of Australia</u>

    <u>coast of New Zealand</u>

    <u>Galapagos Islands</u>

Directions: Think about the passage you read. What was the most important idea? Complete the chart:

Supporting Details

Main Idea

Penguins live in many places throughout the Southern Hemisphere.

- Only two species of penguin live in Antarctica.
- Other penguins live along the coasts of Australia and New Zealand.
- The warmest penguin home of all is the Galápagos Islands.

 Cut out the statements.

Glue them on the chart above to show which is the main idea and which are details.

Dental Health

How many teeth have you lost? Did you know that once your adult teeth grow in, they have to last the rest of your life? That's why it's so important to take good care of your teeth and gums!

Unlike other body parts, <u>a tooth usually can't repair itself.</u> If you get a cavity, a dentist must remove the decayed part and put a filling in its place. That is why it's so important to brush your teeth every day. You also need to take care of your gums. If they get infected, you can lose your teeth. <u>Brushing and flossing daily will keep your gums healthy and prevent halitosis,</u> or bad breath. No one wants dragon breath! These are some reasons you should care for your teeth.

Directions: Read the passage. Answer each question. Underline where you found the answers in the text.

1. A tooth doesn't usually repair itself.

    (a) true)   b) false

2. What can you do to prevent halitosis?

    <u>brushing and flossing daily</u>

Directions: Think about the passage you read. What was the most important idea? Complete the chart:

Supporting Details

Main Idea

It is important to take good care of your teeth and gums.

- Unlike other body parts, a tooth usually can't repair itself.
- If your gums get infected, you can lose your teeth.
- Brushing and flossing will keep your gums healthy and prevent halitosis.

 Cut out the statements.

Glue them on the chart above to show which is the main idea and which are details.

Our Sun

Everyone knows that the sun gives us light. But did you know that the sun makes life possible? Every living thing on Earth relies on the sun.

The sun produces heat that keeps the Earth at the correct temperature. Without the sun, all of the water on Earth would be frozen. Plants and animals must have water to survive. Plants also need sunlight to form glucose which they use for food. As a plant produces glucose, it gives off oxygen. This is released into the air for us to breathe. Finally, the sun creates gravity that keeps the Earth and all of the other planets in orbit. Without the sun, our solar system would not exist.

Directions: Read the passage. Answer each question. Underline where you found the answers in the text.

1. The sun gives off oxygen.

    a) true   (b) false)

2. Explain a way plants use sunlight that helps humans:

    Plants use sunlight to form glucose. As it produces glucose, it gives off oxygen which we breathe.

15

Directions: Think about the passage you read. What was the most important idea? Complete the chart:

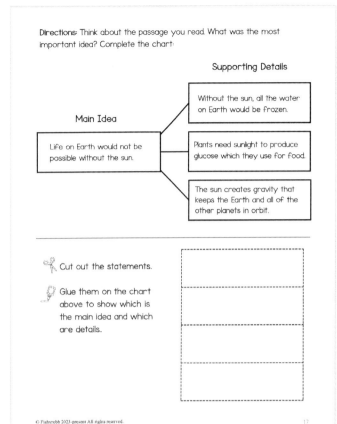

Supporting Details

Main Idea

Main Idea	Supporting Details
Life on Earth would not be possible without the sun.	Without the sun, all the water on Earth would be frozen.
	Plants need sunlight to produce glucose which they use for food.
	The sun creates gravity that keeps the Earth and all of the other planets in orbit.

✂ Cut out the statements.

🖊 Glue them on the chart above to show which is the main idea and which are details.

17

Pioneer Life

Today, most children go to school during the day and play with their friends when they get home. On the weekend, they might participate in sports, go to the movies, or play video games. But life was not like that during pioneer times.

Many pioneer children learned at home instead of going to school. They woke up early and had to help with chores most of the day. Girls helped cook, clean, and sew, and took care of younger siblings. Boys helped their fathers chop wood, build, hunt, and farm. Unlike today, there was no television or video games. Pioneer children had to make their own fun – but only after their work was done.

Directions: Read the passage. Answer each question. Underline where you found the answers in the text.

1. Most pioneer children were schooled at home.

    (a) true)   b) false

2. What sentence shows that in pioneer times work came before play?

    Pioneer children had to make their own fun – but only after their work was done.

19

Directions: Think about the passage you read. What was the most important idea? Complete the chart:

Supporting Details

Main Idea

Main Idea	Supporting Details
Childhood during pioneer times was very different than it is today.	Many pioneer children learned at home instead of going to school.
	They had to wake up early and help with chores most of the day.
	Unlike today, there was no television or video games.

✂ Cut out the statements.

🖊 Glue them on the chart above to show which is the main idea and which are details.

21

Helen Keller

<u>When Helen Keller was born, she was a strong and healthy baby.</u> But as a young child, Helen fell ill. The sickness left her blind and deaf. Learning was difficult for Helen. She could not communicate at all.

A woman named Anne Sullivan became her teacher. With Anne's help, Helen learned to use a special kind of sign language. She also learned to read Braille. <u>Helen was a fast learner. She eventually went to college and was the first deaf-blind person to earn a bachelor's degree.</u> She also learned four languages. As an adult, Helen wrote many books and spoke out about the rights of disabled people. Helen became an inspiration for many.

Directions: Read the passage. Answer each question. Underline where you found the answers in the text.

1. Helen was born blind.

   a) true   (b) false

2. What did Helen achieve that had never been done by a deaf and blind person?

   She was the first deaf-blind person to

   earn a bachelor's degree.

Directions: Think about the passage you read. What was the most important idea? Complete the chart:

Supporting Details

Main Idea

Helen Keller overcame her disability and became an inspiration to others.

- Helen learned a special kind of sign language and how to read Braille.
- She also learned four languages.
- Helen wrote many books and spoke out about the rights of the disabled.

✂ Cut out the statements.

🖊 Glue them on the chart above to show which is the main idea and which are details.

Directions: Read each passage. Underline or highlight the detail that does not support the main idea.

Main Idea: Dolphins are mammals.

You might think a dolphin is a kind of fish but it is actually a mammal. Dolphins have lungs just like you. They must come to the surface to breathe air. A baby dolphin, called a calf, drinks its mother's milk. Dolphins are warm-blooded animals, while fish are cold-blooded. <u>Dolphins can also swim up to 20 miles per hour.</u> Finally, dolphins have a small amount of hair on their bodies.

Main Idea: Many products can be made from corn.

Corn is one of the most popular vegetables to eat, but it can be used for more than just food. Corn is an ingredient in many everyday products like glue and lipstick. It is used to make ethanol which is added to gasoline. <u>However, ethanol is not good for the environment.</u> Hand soaps and toothpaste both have corn-based ingredients. Believe it or not, corn is even used in the production of baby diapers!

Directions: Read each passage. Underline or highlight the detail that does not support the main idea.

Main Idea: Spiders are not insects.

Many people are surprised to learn that spiders are arachnids, not insects. They are different in several ways. An insect has six legs while spiders have eight. <u>Spiders live on every continent except Antarctica.</u> Although most insects have wings and can fly, spiders do not. Another difference is the number of body parts. Insects have three while spiders only have two.

Main Idea: Sofia is a talented musician.

Some people know how to play an instrument but my friend, Sofia, can play four. She plays flute, cello, piano, and guitar. She also sings in the school chorus and writes her own music. Last year, Sofia won the school talent show when she sang one of the songs she wrote. Besides performing, Sofia also gives lessons to her friends. <u>Even though she is busy, Sofia still makes time for her favorite sport, soccer.</u>

Directions: Read each passage. Underline or highlight the detail that does not support the main idea.

Main Idea: Benjamin Franklin was a great inventor.

Benjamin Franklin, one of our founding fathers, was also an inventor. Franklin lived in Philadelphia, Pennsylvania. One of his inventions that is used by many people today is bifocal eye-glasses. He also invented a stove for cooking, and swimming paddles that are similar to swim fins. Have you ever noticed the odometer in your parent's car that tells how far you've driven? That's a Ben Franklin invention too!

Main Idea: Sacagawea helped Lewis and Clark on their journey.

When Lewis and Clark explored the west for President Jefferson, they took along a young Native American named Sacagawea. She helped translate for them when they met Indian tribes. She also helped guide the explorers through the mountains along paths she knew well. Sacagawea had a baby during the expedition. When the group needed more horses, Sacagawea arranged to buy them from her brother, the tribe's chief.

Directions: Read each passage. Underline or highlight the detail that does not support the main idea.

Main Idea: Logan is afraid of heights.

My brother, Logan, is afraid of heights. He starts to shake whenever we have to ride in an elevator. He avoids climbing on ladders, even to get on my bunk bed. Logan misses a lot of fun because of his fear. He refuses to ride the Ferris wheel or roller coaster at the fair. He will not climb trees with me and our friends. He has been afraid of heights since he was three years old. Logan is two years younger than me.

Main Idea: The hippopotamus is extremely dangerous.

Did you know that the hippopotamus is the most dangerous land animal in Africa? They are huge, aggressive, and territorial. A hippo can run up to 30 miles per hour and will charge anyone who threatens it. Their huge teeth, weighing six pounds each, can easily crush anything they bite. Hippos are herbivores and eat only plants. Almost 3,000 people are killed by wild hippos each year.

Directions: Read each passage. Underline or highlight the detail that does not support the main idea.

Main Idea: Car racing requires a lot of safety equipment.

Racecar drivers must protect themselves by using proper safety equipment. Otherwise, a high-speed accident can be deadly. Racing is an exciting sport! A helmet protects the driver's head and face. A special fireproof suit and gloves are worn in case the car catches fire. Today, race cars are equipped with HANS devices. This is a special harness that keeps the head and neck still during a wreck.

Main Idea: Video games have changed a lot over the years.

Kids in the early 1970s had to visit an arcade to play video games. Home video games didn't exist until a few years later. One of the first home games was called Pong. It was very simple compared to the games of today. Players had to hit a little ball with a paddle. Video games now are much more advanced. Many of them look like movies with lifelike characters and actions. Super Mario is a very popular game for kids.

Directions: Read each passage. Underline or highlight the detail that does not support the main idea.

Main Idea: The U.S. has three branches of government.

The United States government is divided into three main parts called branches. The legislative branch creates our laws. The judicial branch interprets our laws. The executive branch enforces them. A system of checks and balances makes sure these three branches have equal power and work together. In the United States, adults have the right to vote. All three parts of our government are based in Washington D.C.

Main Idea: Disney World is a popular vacation spot.

Every year more than 20 million people visit the Magic Kingdom at Disney World. Some of them travel thousands of miles to spend their vacation at "The Happiest Place on Earth." Disney World opened in Florida in 1971. It is the most visited amusement park in the world. People of all ages love the rides and shows which makes it the ideal spot for a family trip. Some people even go back more than once!

Camping

Main Idea	Main Idea	Main Idea
It's important to bring the right equipment when you go camping.	Camping is a perfect activity for people who like outdoor recreation.	Camping in a tent is better than using a camper.
If you plan to cook over a fire, be sure to have matches or a lighter.	Many campsites are near lakes or rivers where you can fish or swim.	It's more expensive to rent a site with camper hookups than it is a tent.
It can be very dark in the woods at night, so you will want a flashlight.	There are many kinds of birds at a campsite for bird watchers to enjoy.	You can fit a tent right into your car trunk.
There can be a lot of insects around, so don't forget bug repellant.	You can go hiking during the day to see nature and get some exercise.	Sleeping in a tent is almost like sleeping outside.

Cut out the statements below. Glue them under the main idea that they support on the chart above.

Bees

Main Idea	Main Idea	Main Idea
A hive has several types of bees that perform different jobs.	Bees can be a valuable part of a farm.	Not all bees are dangerous.
Some worker bees are nurses who take care of newly hatched larvae.	For many crops to grow, the flowers must first be pollinated by bees.	Carpenter bees are very large, but the males can't sting.
Drones are male bees that mate with the queen.	Bees produce honey that can be sold at the market.	Most bees are not aggressive. They only sting if you disturb them.
Collecting food and taking care of the hive is done by worker bees.	Bees pollinate clover and and other plants that are grown to feed livestock.	Some species of bees have a very small stinger that doesn't even work.

Cut out the statements below. Glue them under the main idea that they support on the chart above.

Pets

Main Idea	Main Idea	Main Idea
Some pets are easier to care for than others.	A pet can be more than just a friend.	Having a pet is good for your health.
Dogs need to be trained, walked, and groomed regularly.	Pets can be trained to help the disabled with everyday tasks.	Pets can help you relax and give you a feeling of well-being.
Cats are very easy to litter box train and don't mind being left alone.	A pet can help protect your home from intruders.	Children with pets have a lower chance of having allergies.
Betta fish need just a small bowl and a sprinkle of food each day.	Dogs are often used to guard livestock on farms and ranches.	Having a pet has been proven to lower your blood pressure.

Cut out the statements below. Glue them under the main idea that they support on the chart above.

Stars

Main Idea	Main Idea	Main Idea
The sun is the center of our solar system.	Scientists use special tools to study stars.	There are different types of stars.
All the planets in our solar system revolve around one star – our sun.	Astronomers long ago and today use star charts to map star locations.	Our sun is not the largest or hottest star. It is a medium size yellow star.
The planets get heat and light from the sun. Its gravity holds them in place.	A reflector telescope bounces starlight through mirrors.	The largest star, called a hypergiant, is 1,700 times bigger than our sun.
It takes Earth 365 days to orbit the sun. Jupiter takes 12 years!	Radio telescopes use radio waves to show stars in great detail.	Stars can be blue, white, yellow, or red. Blue stars are the hottest.

Cut out the statements below. Glue them under the main idea that they support on the chart above.

Made in United States
Orlando, FL
08 November 2024